Families

Family
Celebrations

Debbie Gallagher

 **Marshall Cavendish**
Benchmark
New York

This edition first published in 2009 in the United States of America by Marshall Cavendish Benchmark.

Marshall Cavendish Benchmark
99 White Plains Road
Tarrytown, NY 10591
www.marshallcavendish.us

All Internet sites were available and accurate when sent to press.

First published in 2008 by
MACMILLAN EDUCATION AUSTRALIA PTY LTD
15–19 Claremont St, South Yarra 3141

Visit our Web site at www.macmillan.com.au or go directly to www.macmillanlibrary.com.au

Associated companies and representatives throughout the world.

Library of Congress Cataloging-in-Publication Data

Gallagher, Debbie, 1969-
    Family celebrations / by Debbie Gallagher.
        p. cm. — (Families)
    Includes index.
    ISBN 978-0-7614-3133-6
    1. Family—Juvenile literature. 2. Family festivals—Juvenile literature. 3. Anniversaries—Juvenile literature. I. Title.
    HQ744.G33 2008
394.2—dc22

                                                                2008001659

Edited by Georgina Garner
Text and cover design by Christine Deering
Page layout by Raul Diche
Photo research by Brendan Gallagher

Printed in the United States

Acknowledgments
The author and the publisher are grateful to the following for permission to reproduce copyright material:

Cover photograph: Family celebrating a birthday © Getty Images/Jenny Acheson

Photos courtesy of: Blend Stock Photos, 5, 23; Corbis Royalty Free, 21; Digital Vision, 3, 19; © Gingellen/Dreamstime.com, 13; © Hallgerd/Dreamstime.com, 18; © Iofoto/Dreamstime.com, 22; © Razvanjp/Dreamstime.com, 7; © Getty Images/Jenny Acheson, 1; © Getty Images/Frederic J. Brown/AFP, 25; © Getty Images/China Photos, 20; © Getty Images/Digital Vision, 12; © Getty Images/Reza, 24; © Getty Images/Maria Stenzel, 15; © Getty Images/Jung Yeon-Je/AFP, 27; © Ronnie Comeau/iStockphoto, 4; © Terry Healy/iStockphoto, 9; Legendimages, 28; Alan Benson/Lonely Planet Images, 11; Photo-Easy.com, 29; Photos.com, 6; © iofoto/Shutterstock, 26; © Eric Limon/Shutterstock, 14; © Dóri O'Connell/Shutterstock, 8; © PhotoCreate/Shutterstock, 10; © tomediacom/Shutterstock, 17; © wheatley/Shutterstock, 16.

1 3 5 6 4 2

Contents

Glossary words

When a word is printed in **bold**, you can look up its meaning in the Glossary on page 31.

Families

Families live in countries all around the world. Some of your friends may have a family just like yours. Some of your friends may have families very different from yours.

A family shares a special dinner together.

Family celebrations are important to families. Sometimes they are times for the family to have fun together. Sometimes they are times to be thoughtful and to remember the past.

Birthday parties bring family members together to celebrate.

Family Celebrations

There are many types of family celebrations. Some events, such as birthdays, are often celebrated with the family. Other events are celebrated by all the families in a **community.**

Some family events are celebrated by eating a special meal together.

Some family celebrations follow **traditions** and customs. It may be traditional to wear certain clothes at a family celebration.

In Japan, it is traditional for female guests to wear kimonos to weddings.

Births

The birth of a baby is a time of great celebration for a family. Parents, grandparents, brothers, sisters, uncles, aunts, and cousins join in celebrating this happy time.

A sister likes to spend time with her new brother.

Many families celebrate the naming of a baby. **Jewish** babies are named in special **ceremonies**. Some **Christian** families name new babies in front of their church community during a **christening**.

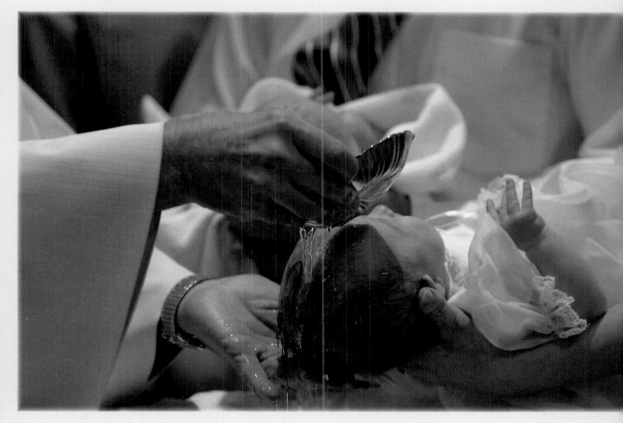

A baby is sprinkled with water at a christening.

Birthdays and Name Days

Many families around the world celebrate the **anniversary** of the day a family member was born. These anniversaries are called birthdays.

Often, a special cake with candles is shared by a family at a birthday party.

In some **cultures**, families celebrate name days. Names are linked to a day of the year. When someone's name is the same as the name day, everyone celebrates.

In Greek families, name days are celebrated by inviting family and friends to a special meal.

Coming-of-age Celebrations

A coming-of-age celebration marks the time when a child grows up. Many families celebrate with a special party when a child turns eighteen or twenty-one.

A Jewish family celebrates when a boy turns thirteen.

For many families, it is very important that their children receive an education. Families often celebrate when their children finish school or college.

A graduation ceremony celebrates the end of a stage in a person's education.

Deaths

Funerals are a time for a family to **mourn** the death of a loved one. Memories of happy times spent together are shared during a funeral.

Flowers are laid on a grave to honor a person who has died.

Many cultures have a special day when families remember their **ancestors**. Families visit graves or **tombs**. They show respect for their ancestors by practicing **rites.**

Chinese families celebrate Tomb Sweeping Day each year by taking care of their ancestors' tombs.

Christmas

Christian families around the world celebrate Christmas. Christmas Day is on December 25. People spend weeks preparing for this important event.

Children get ready for Christmas Day by preparing treats to eat.

Families decorate their homes, buy gifts, and plan special family meals or **feasts**. It is traditional for family members to get together for Christmas dinner.

Pulling holiday crackers at the table is a Christmas tradition for some families.

Id al-Fitr

Id al-Fitr is an important **Muslim** celebration. It celebrates the end of **Ramadan**. It is also a time to celebrate family, friends, and good things that have happened.

During Ramadan, the end of the day is celebrated with a special family dinner.

For Id al-Fitr, people decorate their homes with lights. People dress up in new clothes. Visiting friends and the **extended family** is very important during this time.

Children are given treats and small amounts of money as gifts at Id al-Fitr.

Thanksgiving

Thanksgiving is an important family celebration in the United States. The whole family gets together to give thanks for everything they have.

Some families watch the Thanksgiving Day football game together.

Grandparents, aunts, uncles, cousins, and other relations get together to share a traditional Thanksgiving feast.

A roast turkey is often served at the Thanksgiving meal.

Chinese New Year

Many families celebrate Chinese New Year. This is in January or February each year. Usually, the whole family gets together for a traditional meal.

A traditional Chinese New Year dinner has ten courses and includes fish.

At Chinese New Year, family members often give each other special gifts of money. They visit the oldest members of the family to show respect to them.

Families watch the Chinese New Year parade together.

Mother's and Father's Days

In communities around the world, Mother's Day is a special event each year. It is a day to honor mothers.

Flowers are a traditional gift on Mother's Day.

Some communities also celebrate Father's Day. Korean families celebrate Parents' Day, and they also celebrate Children's Day.

A mother celebrates Children's Day with her sons.

Traditional Costumes

Often, families dress up in costumes for a celebration. For some festivals, family members wear traditional costumes.

In Venice, Italy, children and adults dress up in old-fashioned clothes to celebrate Carnevale.

In Peru, family members wear traditional costumes to celebrate special community events. One of these events is the Festival of Traditional Dance.

This girl in Cusco, Peru, is wearing a style of costume that is hundreds of years old.

A Family Calendar

Birthdays, dinners, and other special events can be marked on a family calendar.

Try this!

Make a calendar and write in all the special events your family will celebrate this month.

January

SUNDAY	MONDAY	TUESDAY	WEDNESDAY	THURSDAY	FRIDAY	SATURDAY
				1	2	3 Grandfather's 80th birthday
4	5	6	7	8 Family dinner	9	10
11	12	13	14 My birthday	15	16	17 Michael's football championship
18	19	20	21	22	23 Kim and Lee's wedding	24
25	26	27	28	29	30	31

Glossary

ancestors	family members who lived in the past
anniversary	the date of a particular event each year
ceremonies	formal occasions that have an important purpose
christening	a Christian ceremony where a child is given a name
Christian	belonging to the Christian religion
community	a group of people living in an area who are connected by culture or identity
cultures	groups of people with the same traditions and practices
extended family	all the members of a family, not just the parents and children
feasts	meals that have a lot of very good food
Jewish	belonging to the religion or being part of the culture of Judaism
mourn	to be sad about the death of a person
Muslim	belonging to the religion of Islam
Ramadan	a month during the year when Muslims avoid eating and drinking from dawn to sunset
rites	religious ceremonies or acts
tombs	burial places
traditions	beliefs, stories, or practices that have been followed by a group of people over time

Index